Home Field

Other Books by Thomas Reynolds:

Small Town Rodeos
The Kansas Hermit Poems
Ghost Town Almanac
Electricity

Copyright 2019

ISBN: 978-0-9987003-4-2
Library of Congress: 2018965110

Book Editor: Gary Lechliter
Formatting: Pam LeRow
Front Cover/Back Cover Images: pixabay.com

Woodley Memorial Press

Acknowledgments

Aethlon: The Journal of Sport Literature (XIII: Spring 1996)
    "Report From the Battle"
Aethlon: The Journal of Sport Literature (XVIII: 1, Fall 1999)
    "Three Versions of Cap Evans' Pool Hall"
Aethlon: The Journal of Sport Literature (XXI: 2, Spring 2004)
    "Rodeo"
Aethlon: The Journal of Sport Literature (XXII: 2, Spring 2005)
    Strip Pit Fishing"
Aethlon: The Journal of Sport Literature (XXIII: 2, Spring 2006)
    "Rock Climbing in Horse Thief Canyon"
Aethlon: The Journal of Sport Literature (XXIV: 1; Fall 2006//Winter 2007)
    "Track Season"
Aethlon: The Journal of Sport Literature (XXV: 1, Fall 2007/Winter 2008)
    "The Bus Ride Home"
Aethlon: The Journal of Sport Literature (XXVI: 2; Spring/Summer 2009)
    "Swim Meet"
Aethlon: The Journal of Sport Literature (XXVIII: 1, Fall 2010/Winter 2011)
    "Prairie Swimmer
Aethlon: The Journal of Sport Literature (XXVIII: 2, Spring/Summer 2011)
    "Pre-Season
Aethlon: The Journal of Sport Literature (XXIX: 1, Fall 2011/Winter 2012)
    "Running Across Chase County, Kansas"
Aethlon: The Journal of Sport Literature (XXX: 2, Spring 2013/Summer 2013)
    "Final Season of the Six-Man Red Dogs"
    "29 Miles"
    "Friday Night Football"
    "Makeup Rodeo"
    "Bike Race"
Aethlon: The Journal of Sport Literature (XXXI: 2 Spring 2014/Summer 2014)
    "Ump"
Aethlon: The Journal of Sport Literature (XXXIII: 2, Spring 2016/Summer 2016)
    "Minor League"
    "State Championship Football Fans"
Aethlon: The Journal of Sport Literature (XXXIV: 1, Fall 2016/Winter 2017)
    "Cage Fighter"
Apple Valley Review (Volume 2, No. 2, Fall 2007)
    "Punch"
The I-70 Review (Summer/Fall 2014)
    "Black Ball Cap"

The Journal (Volume, Issue 3, Fall 2016)
    "Strip Pit Fishing II"
ken*again: the literary magazine (Fall 2007)
    "Chicago Marathon—1999"
New Verse News (November 28, 2008)
    "Venison"
Spitball: The Baseball Literary Magazine (Fall 2018)
    "Wamego Wolverines"
Sport Literate (Volume 7, Issue 1, 15th Anniversary Issue)
    "Mile Run"
Sport Literate (2015)
    "Bus Driver"
Sport Literate (Volume 10, Issue 2, 2017)
    "Radio Play by Play"
    "Sports Reporters"
Stymie: A Journal of Sport and Literature (June 26, 2013)
    "Demolition Derby Car"
Stymie: A Journal of Sport and Literature (March 15, 2013)
    "Post Season"

The following poems were included in *Ghost Town Almanac*, published by Woodley Memorial Press in 2008.

"Strip Pit Fishing I"
"Rock Climbing in Horse Thief Canyon"
"Report From the Battle"
"Three Versions of Cap Evans' Pool Hall"
"Rodeo"

"Fishing on the Kaw River Rule" was included in *Electricity,* a chapbook published by Ligature Press in 1987.

Twenty of these poems were included in *Small Town Rodeos,* a chapbook published by Spartan Press in 2016.

"Venison" was nominated for a 2009 Pushcart Prize by *New Verse News*.

Table of Contents

I. Pre-Season

Pre-Season 3
Flint Hills Runner 5
Track Season 6
Venison 8
Duck Calls 10
Stadium 11
Earhart and Howland Island 12
Running and Poetry 13
Cross-Country Run 15
Reunion 18
Things We Share with Our Small Town Rivals 20
Osawatomie Football Stadium 21
Knute Rockne's Plane 22

II. The Season Begins

Makeup Rodeo 25
Friday Night Football 26
Allen Fieldhouse Mop-Up Girl 28
Seventh Grade Track Practice 29
March Track Meet 31
Disqualified Second Heat Hurdler 32
Punch 33
"Beat the Bulldogs!" 34
Sports Reporter 35
Keeping Score 36
Bruce Whaley Spirit Ride 38
Minor League 43
The Lonely Circle 44
Report from the Battle 45
Wamego Wolverines 46
Mile Run 48

III. Mid-Season

Swim Meet 53
Strip Pit Fishing I 55
Prairie Swimmer 56
Three Versions of Cap Evans' Pool Hall 58
Trophy 60
Cage Fighter 62
Upper Deck 64
Ump 65
Rock Climbing in Horse Thief Canyon 66
Rebuilding Coach 67
Bus Driver 68
Shadow Cyclist 70
Fishing on the Kaw River Rule 71
Running Across Chase County, Kansas 72

IV. The Season Ends

Chicago Marathon—1999 77
What Losing Sounds Like 78
Final Season of the Six-Man Red Dogs 79
Rodeo Clown 81
1600 Meter Final 83
Radio Play by Play 84
Strip Pit Fishing II 85
State Championship Football Fans 87
Playoff Momentum After a Lopsided Loss 88
The Bus Ride Home 89
Chiefs Games 91
October 92
The End 93

V. Post-Season

Post Season 97
Home Field 99
Black Ball Cap 100
Bike Race 101
Tossing Stones 102

Russell Field 103
Walking the Field After Last Night's Win 104
Legacy 105
Driving Range: Web.Com Tour 106
Globe 108
Rodeo 110
Fleet of Foot 111
Souvenir Baseball 113
Demolition Derby Car 114

Home Field

**Poems by
Thomas Reynolds**

For Ruby, Audrey, and Rachel

I. Pre-Season

Pre-Season

Baseball

Turning the ball seam
Over seam in his hand,

Searching for the feel
That deserted him last May.

Football

The new coach gazes through
Fogged lenses in the parking lot

As the reserve cornerback first
Pain-tests the injured knee.

Fishing

Late February afternoon.
The old farmer's boots

Crackle on ice
He gauges between two fingers.

Swimming

She finds herself walking
The mile to school with heavy limbs

As if underwater,
Testing the resistance.

Golf

She now takes to reading
In their son's old room

While he putts into a coffee mug,
Cursing his soft, unsteady grip.

Basketball

Blast his short, stubby legs
Only good enough for JV,

Hands nimble
As a catcher's mitt.

Cross Country

He doesn't even need to breathe
Across Kansas hills,

His mind empty as a ravine
In the Zen of his dream.

Tennis

One can only practice serves
Against the fence for so long

With gloved hands gripping
A lime-green rock that barely bounces.

Track and Field

Pretending the snow-topped fence post
At the end of the pasture

Leads after ten laps,
With only one more lap to go.

Flint Hills Runner

I.
All day wind
Sprints through

Grass and never
Gets out of breath.

II.
At night no one to play
Catch with or run

For a pass unless
You count the stars.

III.
At dawn it races
For the hilltop

Before sun leans across
That gray ribbon of creek.

IV.
Who can explain
Something so ancient,

That seeps from rocks,
And rises from earth?

V.
The old rancher
Stands at his barn

Watching for what
Chases that old boy.

Track Season

On the empty track
Under a January sky,
My daughter grows smaller.

I watch from the stands,
From the highest bleacher,
Her first tentative preparations.

Even as she pushes herself
Faster and faster toward the line
On the far side of the stadium,

I see her as growing smaller,
Sprinting back into childhood,
Until she makes the turn

And becomes thirteen again,
Legs petrifying in the cold,
Arms churning but measured,

Head committed. Maybe life already
Picked the winners. Dodge balls
Missile-seek her forehead,

Propelled by the strongest arms.
Basketballs in her hands resist
Predictability, caressing

Air, but rarely hoops.
In the process of selection,
Like me, she'll never be first.

Inexorable laws. But still
She keeps running, plumes
Of breath trailing her wake

As she begins another lap,
My heart running its own race
As I listen to the crowd erupt.

Dry leaves stir like banners,
Wind whistles through railing,
And dead weeds do the wave.

Venison

My ancestors were hunters,
Walking wooded paths at dusk.

Hogs were slaughtered beyond flower beds,
And amidst carnage, people gossiped about weddings.

So when my brother the hunter brought venison steaks
To be cooked with turkey and ham on Thanksgiving,

That was only fitting.
We leaned over as they sizzled on the stove,

Detecting wildness unloosed--
Rain dripping from pines, piles of moldy leaves,

The bite of first snow in the air,
Hedge smoke drifting from a distant line shack.

My brother recounted the hunt in western Missouri,
How the doe trailed off for miles after she was shot,

Finally falling beside a stand of scrub oak.
My brother and others immediately set to with knives,

First dragging her onto a sheet of new fallen snow,
Then slicing her from end to end and removing the heart.

Wind beat against a loose pane in the kitchen window,
And no one even grimaced when her head was removed.

How soon even the skittish settled into the old ways!
The wood in the stove spat sparks onto rugs.

My uncle and a few of the boys stood outside the shed,
Hurling knives into dirt and judging depth.

The two youngest began running through rooms,
With the smallest destined to be shot and quartered.

Deer Boy maintained a step or two until he was cornered,
While all of us smiled to see him die so gracefully.

My aunt handed me a plate of newly thawed venison,
And after laying them in the pan, I stared at my hands.

Dark blood coursed down small rivulets,
While echoes of the night woods encircled me.

Duck Calls

Night is alive with language,
Droning syllables of cicadas.

For a man who has never traveled beyond
Kansas City, four hours from his hometown,

Who scoffs at reading and ignores news
Traveling by satellite from foreign countries,

Places where people are always "them,"
His workshop behind his garage is alive

With foreign tongue, music of sky
And water. At 2 a.m. the universe might

Be listening. The barrel, sounding board,
And reed from his latest instrument

Seem suited to his fingers, his lips.
His entreaties, translated by wood,

Beg to be understood. Sky replies
Through the open window

With silence. Or is it leaning in
With an immigrant's skepticism

To understand his broken syllables,
The message he can't quite form—

"Come closer. I'm your friend."

Stadium

It rises from the hillside like an enormous bowl,
Open to clouds, prepared to be filled.

Sky offers only wind sweeping across grass,
Across dense trees to north and west,

Scattering snow among blue and red seats,
Flecking turf with flakes running sprints.

Somewhere loose bolts strain to keep one
Top row seat from leaping up and shouting.

By mid-morning snow is thinning.
The only thing stirring is a pigeon

Strutting atop the press box
Carrying a stick and piece of string.

Leaning over the railing makes my head
Light like a flag whipping atop the pole.

Who knew the universe was so empty,
So hungry, when this was only woods

Rising up and scattered with stones,
Now a monument to need, to love.

Earhart and Howland Island

July 2, 1937

Scattered clouds cast shadows on the ocean surface
As she scanned horizon for tiny Howland Island,

Only a land sliver where Coast Guard cutter
Itasca waited to provide refueling, receiving her calls

But responding with messages she couldn't hear.
The Electra was then flying at 7000 feet, as she radioed

Itasca in a calm voice "must be on you but cannot see u,"
Cloud shadows perhaps making the island difficult to spot.

She was likely leaning forward, in the cockpit as in life,
With "a delicate touch on the stick," scanning horizon

As navigator Fred Noonan gripped a wrinkled chart,
Silently attempting another calculation,

Yet requiring Itasca's lost signals to establish direction.
We leave them there: Earhart sending signals

Progressively garbled, broken by static,
The plane's gas dropping precipitously, while ahead ocean

And sky battled for dominance, in the way Atchison's
Rock-strewn glacier-carved rolling hills sparred with blue sky.

Thoughts perhaps returned to Kansas, childhood play
With sister Pidge, their incessant appetite for adventure,

Homemade ramp secured to the toolshed roof, venturing
Into open space for the first time in a wood box that

No matter how she landed—torn dress, bruised hip,
Battered pride—fueled "sensation of exhilaration."

Running and Poetry

Mist is already freezing
As I step onto the street
And test my rhythm.

Just a quick twenty blocks,
A brief rondeau, lethargy and
Common sense negotiating.

Pain just above
The right ankle from my last
Run punctuates each beat.

Headlights approach, then
Veer away, filtering through
Branches of the nearest oak,

Briefly spotlighting
A man in short sleeves
Pacing on the walk.

Image prime for metaphor:
A tiger pacing his cage
With fierce, red eyes.

One hand grips the phone,
The other draws emphatic
Scrawls into air, loops

And flourishes, lined out
So that his two pleas
Echo again and again,

A villanelle about love
And betrayal, until
Darkness erases it all.

I wonder what diction,
What form, my legs and already
Flailing arms scribble onto

The page of an empty street.
Definitely open form,
Beats stopping and starting.

Tonight my running doesn't
Have much to say, nor does
It possess clear means

To express it. It's muddled,
Stumbling, hobbled by ice,
Yet legs keep churning,

Out of habit, out of desire,
Syllable after syllable,
One footfall after another,

Hoping for an epiphany
Sparked by one good stanza
Or at least a decent couplet.

Cross Country Run

Geese

I must run a bit longer.
Morning sky beckons,
Gray and frozen.
An arrow points south
Toward where I know.

Field

Already I feel wind
In the bones of my legs.
Blood swirls up
Like a flock of birds
Scattered in corn.

Levee

Like flood water,
I rise through weeds
To the gravel road,
Course down tire tracks,
Then pour over the other side.

Abandoned Car

I give it a wide berth.
Someone is racing home
To family that long ago
Stopped listening for
His key in the door.

Ravine

I am like blood coursing
Through an artery,

Or a clot making its way
With hard, thumping steps
Toward an unsuspecting heart.

Grass

Like whispering stalks,
I lean forward in the wind
And let it bend me
As if in prayer
To the sky.

Rock Bluff

My passage through
Its life is so brief
I may not exist.
Even my hard steps
Are silent as stone.

Leaves

In gullies
As I climb,
Ghosts lie in wait,
Grabbing my ankles
Rattling tiny bones.

Creek

I hear its muted steps when
All is telling us
Not to run anymore,
Lie still
Among downed branches.

Thicket

From the tangle of bramble
And dead limbs I leave
Behind all which will,
If I fail to run,
Pin and prick me

Reunion

Spinning uphill
On a country highway,
I'm reveling in air.

Scent of grass,
Pine needles, damp
From rain showers.

My feet haven't
Touched ground
Seemingly for years.

Suddenly, a hornet
Pelts my face, crawls
Into my helmet.

My right hand rises.
My left wrenches the handlebars.
Pavement rises

To within a foot
Of my face, and the bike,
Trusted companion,

Bows down to cushion
My fall. All of us embrace,
Old friends making

A scene. We reminisce
Till there's nothing
Left to remember,

Spilling hearts'
Blood, tears,
Till it hurts.

Weeds consorting
With their leader, the wind,
Are the old clique

Who whisper
But never loud
Enough to understand.

I pat the ground
One last time
To wrap things up,

Then bike and me,
We get on
With life.

Things We Share With Our Small Town Rivals

- Dried weeds whipping in cattle pen corners
- Rusted gates open onto empty pastures
- Grass-covered farm roads leading to sagging barns
- Walking paths choked with cottonwood leaves
- Pickup trucks half filled with firewood for winter
- Farm dogs rising from naps sniffing the wind
- Wind rustling corn rows, rattling kitchen windows
- Mothers staring at clouds that look like mountains
- Fathers wandering in footprints of their grandfathers
- Sons tackling that which would keep them here
- Daughters cheering that which might help them escape
- Wind rustling horses' manes, rattling window frames
- Cattle moving slowly in evening back to hay piles
- Sons driving home tired and bruised after football practice
- Daughters driving home with lights on after part-time jobs
- Mothers and fathers resting on cracked kitchen chairs
- Coaches in dark parking lots talking Friday's game
- Wind tearing at jacket collars, at baseball caps
- Enmity lightly tapping at smeared window panes
- Screen doors suddenly blowing open, then slamming shut
- Birds darting in and out of whipping trees
- Foxes standing in weeds glaring at chicken coops
- Black snakes sloughing beneath stone layers
- Bushes bent, branches cracking

Osawatomie Football Stadium

Atop the hill,
You stand above the town,
A beacon for the surrounding flood plain.

In early light,
Your red seats catch fire and blaze.
Does the man on his front steps notice the flames?

From the press box, smudged windows
Gaze at rows of fading homes with peeling paint.
Do future stars sleep behind pulled curtains?

Bolted onto telephone poles
Speakers let action roll without comment,
Grass tufts and black beetles vying for supremacy.

On the top row facing east,
Past the town, miles of dense grass, the swollen creek,
I envision only waving pennants and red jackets.

From the alley a woman shouts obscenities at her man,
Yet I imagine only cheers and clapping hands,
Drum cadences, blaring horns.

Through varnished seats,
In dried leaves gathered in clumps beside steps,
I smell regret, melancholy, elation.

Beneath your network of iron, your wide beams,
I sense the solidarity of competition,
Reinforced mettle that can only be pride.

The scoreboard is so exultant it refuses to keep score,
Touchdown after touchdown by wind
So fleet of foot across the field.

Knute Rockne's Plane

March 31, 1931

[Easter] Heathman, a witness to the crash, was the memorial's caretaker for decades before he died in 2008 at the age of 90." -- Kansas City Star

The site in rolling prairie two miles from Bazaar, Kansas,
Tried not to call attention to itself.

Perhaps cattle lowed softly or rattled bells.
Killdeer might have called shrilly to distract

Predators from eggs nestled in tall grass.
The farm boy who was one of the first on the scene might

Have been whistling a country tune inside the barn,
Dreaming of Babe Ruth, Lou Gehrig, Red Grange.

This landscape, however, savored modesty, stillness.
Edges rounded, open to wind and sky.

So when an engine's roar from the north grew louder,
An explosive crack echoed among rocks as the left wing

Struck the ground, and a thunderous crash as the plane's body
Plummeted upside down through fog splitting damp earth,

Birds and cattle were silenced. Landscape took a moment
To absorb the sound, then Heathman's footfalls

Echoed across the field, jagged stones, burning grass.
How could he have known among bodies strewn almost

In a straight line about the fuselage was that of the coach,
Vibrant leader of men, winner of three championships.

Whose name rang from headlines, whom this space would
Consecrate with bent grass, birdsong, and blue sky.

II. The Season Begins

Make-Up Rodeo

Two hours after heavy rain drove away the crowd,
It resumes in a vacuum, no announcer's patter or glib

Patriotic banter, just clipped pronouncements
Of times, of who has placed, for calf ropers

Gathered in the empty parking lot, barely talking now,
Attempting to stay focused and score checks

Before heading out for the next small county rodeo,
Driving all night in dented trucks, open prairie

Swallowing their headlights, dried weeds
Every hundred miles or so soaking up their pee.

No flag-carrying rodeo gals. No invocations
To the great cowpoke in the sky, roping hearts

Instead of calves. The rodeo clown,
Stretched out across three metal folding chairs,

Has been drained of lewd banter, his lifeblood.
Only gnats cheer on, frenzied by lights.

Darkness leans against a telephone pole
Beyond the last truck and horse trailer.

Listening to the crescendo of exhaustion,
Thundering of empty stands.

Friday Night Football

The horizon glows
West of that small
Gathering of homes.

Something is stirring again,
Seeping through leaves of drying corn,
From tailpipes of abandoned cars,

Through rotting boards
Of collapsed barns,
Across quarry stone.

Lights shine down
To isolate it,
Diagnose it.

A crowd draws round
As if to contain it.
Grass has been shaved

To bare it. Dazzled by fear,
The squeamish
Turn from it.

The cracked surface
Like parched skin
Displays it,

Red and black
In shifting patterns
Flowing in waves,

Finally dissipating
From the prairie's
Pocked skin.

Nothing serious,
Just a vapor,
A tremor,

Something in the air
Stirred by falling leaves
And the first chill wind.

Allen Fieldhouse Mop-Up Girl

You arrive in uniform.
Hallways advise you to buck up.
Frosted windows question your salt, your mettle.

When you approach the court,
Your throat pushes down
This morning's take out.
Your hands embrace, knuckles pop.
Back bends, shoulders straighten.

Five minutes before game time,
You crouch in position five yards from the basket.
You visualize competence, harmony.
Energy flows about you like the water around a stone.

You will not touch court at the whistle.
You must earn it. You must remain alert.
When needed, you leap onto the hardwood.
Graceful, efficient,
You swoop in to acknowledge, adjust, correct.
In the ref's hands, the ball remains at attention.
The goal leans over to praise you.
Lights admire your style, your dedication.

In that moment, you are indispensable.
Even the diehard near the top of the stands knows this.
His complete indifference betrays his confidence.
Your mastery makes you undetectable.
The joker who can't acknowledge this,
Can't embrace your supremacy,
Isn't worthy of your skill,
Your sublime expedition,
Your sweat.

Seventh Grade Track Practice

Sisyphean,
We propelled the boulders
Of our seventh grade selves
Up Wallace Park hill
For two hours every afternoon,
With coach posed nobly near
The abandoned refreshment stand,
Whistle poised like a silver trumpet.

Zeus-like, he seemed then,
To rail-thin, acned pituitary non-marvels.
Although what god, we might have asked,
Wore frayed short pants,
A faded Red Sox cap,
A band of blubber rising
Above a large brown belt.
His spit struck the ground,
However, like lightning bolts.
Perhaps earth shook,
Shuddering waves rising
Though grass blades.

Coach whistled our ascent time and again.
We didn't know what we were being punished for,
Unless it was our utter hopelessness,
Daring to be competent,
Or why, in frustration, he glared into sky,
Adjusting the bill of his cap to divert sun,
Unless somehow we were also his punishment,
Assigned to him willy-nilly,
For being human,
For being a teacher,
For believing in anything so modest
As poised, smooth carriages
From legs and forms like ours.

He was carrying us
Throughout that year,
Even as he closed the classroom door,

Plodded down narrow halls,
Pausing on the front steps to take sips
Of warm cola and groaning,
Let breeze attempt to carry away
Our voices, that later blew in again through
His open window as he stood over his sink,
Washing one cup, a plate, and two pots.

Possibly the whole world was carrying us
Even as we were lifted again and again,
Lain down in tall grass at the top,
At his whistle wheeled down again.
We were ungainly, cumbrous as granite.
We had substance,
Enough to punish some sin the world
Was guilty of, that would require
Penance, tediously repetitious,
Class after class, year after year,
That might never be repaid,
Never be completed.

March Track Meet

The school building tenses,
Poised to run.

Buses arrive, rocked by wind.
Engines race.

Athletes launch themselves into the cold.
Each team stakes out a home.

Like those of pioneers, it is transitory,
Meager, maybe in gravel beneath the stands,

Near weeds beside a ravine, on the south side
Of the restrooms, using walls as wind breaks.

Some stretch in grass. Others keep warm
Jogging laps around the parking lot.

Wind rips away words as they utter them,
Spitting syllables across prairie.

When sun momentarily outpaces
One sprinting black and gray cumulous cloud,

It hurls a narrow shaft of light across the field.
Hills leap out of mist to spot it.

Winding road heaves another bus into the lot,
While jagged, gigantic clouds race across sky.

Disqualified Second Heat Hurdler

Away from the track,
None recognize you,
Missing the subtlety of your fluctuating spark,
The confidence of your unabashed humility,
Your heat, your unchecked hubris,
Your hesitant heroics.

You lower your head
To gain solidity from the ground.
Fine gravel chatters to keep you calm.
Wind attempts to bolster your pride.
That line of trees draws an arrow to your heart.

Movement is required
To keep things still.
Even trampled oak leaves stop you cold.
Even faded signs hold you in place.
You move only as the earth moves.
You grip air to prevent tumbling off.

Stepping onto the empty bus,
You fade into the door's rubber seal.
You slip beneath yellow and white paint.
Dust billowing up from under seats
Gathers you.
You ride on the crest of a used tissue scrap.
You surf on waves of empty space.

Punch

At thirteen, my daughter's friend
Is learning how to box,
Sparring twice a week.

The gym is dim and shadowy.
When she jabs a left hook,
Striking at spinning dust motes,

Her thin arm with extended fist
Becomes a sweeping jackhammer
Traveling the length of the gym.

Sweat beads above her upper lip,
And both eyes remain tightly closed,
But her thoughts are inscrutable.

The boy who taunts her going down,
Or the silence of an empty house,
Steady drip of a leaking faucet.

Whispered encouragement of a father
Whose memory is growing dim,
Dead in a car accident three years ago.

She sidesteps to mat's edge,
And for whatever grips her attention,
Beyond the slamming of some door

Echoing across an empty parking lot,
She unleashes one blistering punch that
Based on her grim smile, seems to land.

"Beat the Bulldogs!"

To the person who climbed
The water tower last night,
Securing a hand-painted banner
From the walkway encircling the tower
Just below the summit,
Your courage and fortitude is laudable,
Ascending the ladder after dark perhaps
With a reluctant friend calling out support,
"Whatever you do, man, don't look down!"
From his position in tall bluegrass whipping
In south wind that above tore at your jacket collar
Attempting to pry hands from the metal bar,
Your head starting to spin as a hawk glided nearby
Nearly motionless while something heavy
And droning slapped your cheek.

How I envy your dedication, you bon vivant,
Your windmill-tilting stab at inspiration,
For a team winless for three seasons.
But more than that, the vista from up there,
After securing the banner with twist-ties,
You sitting on the walkway with your back
Firmly pressed against the tower's outer wall,
With the town where you grew up reduced
To a few flickering street bulbs,
Businesses half-lit, the flashing neon bar sign,
Truck lights peering down some gravel path,
Your friend's wavering calls to come down
Fading in and out through wind gusts
And you too petrified to stretch,
Much less answer him.

Sports Reporter

Tonight is a road game.
Highway unfurls like a banner.
Your red Mazda gut-checks,
Then stutters toward Pomona.

You are alone.
On the passenger seat
Your notebook flutters open, hungry for words.
Pens in the cup holder are goalposts.
Surrounding hills are half-empty stands.

Inside Buzzard's Pizza,
You nod at the hometown fans.
You are odd and awkward
Yet loved in the way peculiar things become fixtures.
You are Grandma's turkey chandelier.
The panther mural on the side of a barn,
The one with crossed eyes and a smirk.
You eat alone at a corner table,
Pencil poised, eager for news bits,
Above yard line markers of your notebook.

On the sidelines, you come alive.
Love pulses in every note jot,
Every photo of helmeted leaps and contested runs.
The dejected kicker, helmet on the ground,
Who just booted another stuttering goose,
Even glances at you in the fourth quarter.
You are in that moment a confidante,
A fellow combatant. Sky says, "You belong,"
Writ across a dark background.
That line of stars is an ellipses.
Goalposts are exclamation marks.

Keeping Score

As always, he sits
Three rows above the team,
Team jacket on, notebook
Open to pages dense
With scribbles, pen
Poised like a javelin.

His father somewhere
Nearby, staring ahead,
As if trying to burn
Some thought from his mind,
Or walking the parking lot
As if prepping his stance
To heave a shotput
Of regret moon-sized
Above the fence
Into dark grass.

Water on the brain,
He'd told someone
Long ago, the mother
Long gone, the beat-up pickup
In the shadows a sign
Of all that had gone wrong
As well as right.

It still runs, pardner,
And that's all the right
A fellow needs.

Once coach was asked
About this most attentive fan.

"Well, if he's writing
Suggestions, Lord knows
I need all the help I can get."

Back in the gym,
It's halftime,

His son is writing
Furiously again, his head
Stuffed with notes,
Tabulating who
Knows what,
Panther jacket
Zipped to the neck,
Hell with the heat.

Once at night,
Heading to the john,
The father spotted
The son's notebook on the floor
Beside the chair.

He didn't open it,
Just stared at it
For a moment
By moonlight.

Bruce Whaley Spirit Ride

1.
Start time.
A few stragglers,
Including me,
Still take inventory
And not just for gear.

2.
All is fluid.
I am one with the bike
And the road.
Or is that two?

3.
Something is working
Itself out of my limbs.
Some buried anger
May be losing its grip.

4.
The rider I pass
Is in this moment
A fellow traveler.
He nods
Almost imperceptibly.

5.
Already the cloud
Jets across my mind's
Mottled sky:
Why am I doing this?

6.
At the midpoint of the hill
I shift:
Gears,
In my seat,
My sense of what I am capable.

7.
It occurs to me I
Must trust these drivers
At my back more
Than anyone I've
Ever known.

8.
When the Ford Escort
Nearly grazes me,
I have a religious experience,
Grinding away in the draft
Of something greater
Than myself.

9.
I don't hear,
Only sense,
The rider behind me
Who becomes the rider in front of me.

10.
Suddenly I am alone.
Even fence posts
Have grown tired of cheering.

11.
Even in the peace
Of this moment
I must look ahead—
And from the corner
Of my left eye—
Behind.

12.
If I live to ninety
This year is the midpoint of my life.
It feels like this—
I think I might survive it
If I just keep pedaling.

13.
Nirvana—
Reaching the hill's summit
Only to spy
A series of steeper hills.

14.
When you focus
On the road just ahead
Of your front wheel,
Your world seems level.

15.
In a gravel drive,
I swallow water
And check the map
For the next turn
I didn't design
But will follow.

16.
Do I prefer edges
Or middles?
The knifepoint
Of beginnings,
Or the dull ache
Of halfway?

17.
My water tastes like plastic,
But the air tastes of pine
And cut grass.
Cheers!

18.
My pace quickens.
I turn onto the last stretch of road
With a shout of encouragement
To gears straining
Inside me.

19.
I'm not pedaling
The afternoon away
But living it
In a way only those ahead
And behind can acknowledge.

20.
After one last hill
I'm now able to breathe
Without thinking about doing so.

21.
I believe in the duality
Of air and spirit—
Headwind and tail.

22.
Tires are singing
Of joy one can know
Only after a long ride
With muscles and blood
Thrumming.

23.
Of this moment
Coursing downhill
I will remember the sense
Of owning nothing,
Not even the bike,
But also everything.

24.
I feel my feet
Spinning in circles
And know that
I'm circling back
To some semblance
Of where I started.

25.
The road will be shaped
By my abilities,
By happenstance,
By wind, sky,
And pedals.

26.
I nearly fall from the bike
As I lean against the car.
Perhaps I've fallen or dived
Or both into something deeper
And wider and more lasting
Than before

27.
I'm floating in it
As I stand here
Beside the truck.

28.
My bike and I
Are two.
But I love how it
Leans against the truck
Just resting.

Minor League

Who can blame the fellow five seats away
And down one row, for being proud, for boasting

His son plays for the Joplin Blasters, the road team,
For turning to us, strangers, and telling us his son

Is the one who turned that double-play, who sliced
That blooper into left field when the rest of the team

Was hapless at the plate, by then down by seven.
"It is amazing" that his son is still playing ball

At twenty-eight, though not tracking
For the majors. "Still playing the game he loves,"

Though in an independent league, team names
Like Airhogs, Railcats, Saltdogs, Wingnuts,

Still chasing down fly balls in the outfield,
Racing to first trying to beat the throw,

Holding on to the dream, still making
A father proud, even one pushing sixty,

Still turning to his neighbors and pointing
His son out as if this were little league,

As if he were young with the whole world
Of what his son might become before him.

The Lonely Circle

Tulsa Elite vs. The Blaze

You embrace the solitude, the independence,
Of the orange clock face encircling your being.
Your pitching arm, wearing down, is the minute hand,
Speeding up game time beneath the July sun,
Now stopping time as you pause before the wind-up,
No clear beginning, middle, or end.

What it shuts out: the voice rising from your gut
That halfway to your throat transforms into a scream.
What it keeps in: all dreams of being strong, whole,
Bold thoughts that try to spin away or evaporate.
The batter drops her right hand and grips the bat.
Her cleats paw at the artificial turf.

You pause four beats longer than seems necessary.
You are the hermit who revels in isolation.
When wind knocks at the cabin door you turn to the wall.
When a group of walkers stroll by you stare into the sun.
Nothing can touch your intricate self-sufficiency.
Your capacity for stillness, your stealth.

Report from the Battle

"Soldiers in both armies played the game,
whenever and wherever they could,
'just like boys,' one of them remembered."

©   Geoffrey C. Ward, *Baseball, An Illustrated History*

Bases are expeditiously positioned across the field,
Three soldierless coats and a knapsack for home.
Choosing sides, we name two teams, West and East,
And establish boundaries: two oaks the foul lines,
And for the home run mark the shallow-dug ravine
Where only lately concluded, more dead were buried.

For both sides, two privates were deemed captains,
Advanced in rank by the quickness of their throws,
The facility of their hands, their killer instinct
Which is, at heart, merely a school-boy's ardor.

The West takes the field, expecting a short recess,
Lining their muskets in the grass for easy access.
Joe Puttnam, their catcher, swings his like a bat,
Launching a perfect ball, he says to all, past center,
Tracing it with his eyes into the Confederate camp
And cringing, as everyone laughs, when it explodes.

Taking the outfield, pummeling his fist in his hand,
Runs Jack Chapman, so adept at bringing down flies
He's called, in the game, "death to flying things."
To the bottom of the fourth the game is scoreless.
Murphy's pitching, and two outs down, faces Miller,
Who lowers his shoulder, rockets a blur to center.

Chapman, going back, raises his arm above his head
When there comes a scattering fire from the north
Of which the three outfielders barehand the brunt.
The left and right revive, but the center is lost,
And fallen near the ravine, will not return home.

Miller is the luckiest, we think, whose certain out
Drops harmlessly onto the burnt grass, a home run.

Wamego Wolverines

Uniforms include wool pants,
White flannel shirts, caps,
And dark knee-high socks.

Players arrive at the field
From neighborhood homes
Dressed for battle.

Full-time manual jobs
At the quarry or factory
Keep them strong and fit.

Some have already stoked
Competitive fires
With whisky and rum.

The hometown Wolverines
Warm up by pitching and catching
Bare-handed.

The ball is yarn wound
Around a rubber core
Covered by horsehide strips.

Pain is inevitable,
So the catcher wraps two rags
Twice round his left hand.

Each shirt has a "W"
Emblazoned on its chest,
But players are known here.

None will be mistaken
For arrogant Red Stockings
From nearby Raleigh.

They will not intentionally
Spike the catcher when
Stealing home plate

Nor trip runners
On their way to second.
They will uphold virtue

And common decency
Except when retaliation
Is just and good.

They will curse only
When called for, then
Apologize later.

They will give townies
As well as those arriving
By team and wagon

From nearby farms,
Some far as twenty miles,
Good reason to cheer,

Gossip and gripe,
Lean back in the sun
And laugh and smile.

Mile Run

Winner:

His parents turn up
Their jacket collars

And congratulate
Their sperm and egg.

Second:

His baby sister sports
A furtive grin

Because he now
Understands her life.

Third:

A medal the size
Of a quarter

For four months
Of torture.

Fourth:

No medal
But a monarch

Lands on his chest
As he lies in the grass.

Fifth, Sixth, Seventh:

Brothers.
Unable to separate,
They move
Elbow to elbow.

Eighth:

A converted
Javelin thrower

Trying hard
To keep the faith.

Ninth:

The sound of the gun
Is like something

From the Old West,
It was so long ago.

Dead Last:

The mother's hand
Moves in slow motion

As she lifts the coffee
All the way to her lips.

III. Mid-Season

Swim Meet

On her haunches,
She squats poolside,
And without recognition,

Stares as I pass.
The mole on her cheek
Pulses with her heart.

Goggle straps behind
Her ears bob like
Wind-blown skin flaps.

Her frog skin suit
Pulls taut beneath her arms
As she grows larger,

Her arms no longer stiff,
Dipping one hand
With fingers spread

Into the water's skein,
Slipping soundless
Above her head

And in a split second,
She sees webbing
Between digits

Resist the wind,
While recognition
Leaps into her eyes.

Who says no parental
Urge stirs within us
On the still banks,

Waiting in grass,
Our limbs already tired,
Our world growing dim,

As small ones among us
Spring as if from some call,
Leaping into waves,

Flashing, indistinguishable,
Lurching forward
With spasmodic gulps,

Eventually crawling
From ancient waters
Victorious onto dry land.

Strip Pit Fishing I

Near Pleasanton,
The strip pits of a defunct coal-mining operation,
Hidden from the road by thick woods
And tall rock fences,
Grow darker with every rain,
Every avalanche of dirt and rock
From towering walls.
Dynamite blasts,
Nearly fifty years old,
Still echo from the rock bluffs,
And small reverberations
Still send fragments
Scurrying into the deep pits.

We drive these roads,
Scarred by wheels of coal trucks,
Through stinkweed,
Down the only level approach to the water.
Lowering the boat,
We coast onto the choppy surface,
Marred by wind,
And maneuver around the crooked fingers
Of the pit's edge.
The steady rumble of the motor
Crawls along the cliffs,
As if another boat follows our movements
From the opposite shore.

We don't catch anything.
The bass hide among the drowned rocks,
Prowling secret hollows.
When they surface,
Finally arisen in death,
It won't be our hooks
Their scaly jaws grasp.
When we lower the anchor,
The endless expanse of rope,
It goes down, down,
And dangles above the bottom.

Prairie Swimmer

Womb

In pulsings of
Amniotic waves, she kicked in place,
Flipping fins with digits extended.

Tide

Belly down on blue-green
Seaweed tangles of the living room floor,
Like an upturned turtle,
She waited for the tide
To carry her to the sea.

River

She points to the rock shaped like a platform
At the promontory tip and lowers goggles
Over spot-flecked skin,
Above goldfish eyes.
Frog-like, she leaps.

Winter

Walking the fencerow over frozen ground,
She tests her arms against the March wind,
One over the other
In a tight front crawl,
Racing for the gate.

Meet

Under the surface she becomes
Like the rest something other, a creature
Who senses some ancient tug

In the cells of her hands,
In her lungs.

Body

Her body is 70 percent water.
She is a small, compact lake
Into which swimmers dive from a bluff
And do laps around the thirty percent island
Guarded by a chain-link fence.

Prairie

After a swim in the creek,
Running in lush grass cresting above her head
White-capped by wind,
She leaps above waves
As if lunging for air
Before diving below again.

Sea

She paddles in a pond
Surrounded by rolling hills,
Once the bed of an ancient inland sea.
In mist, ghost fish
glide above her.

Pond

Tethys, Greek goddess of earth's fresh waters,
Was mother to three thousand daughters.
One now wades ashore
From the blinding surface,
Returning to this life.

Three Versions of Cap Evans' Pool Hall

Marion, Kansas. 1904.

The first is sketchy, zeroing in on angles
Of the narrow building, looking from the extreme
Right front corner, diagonally to opposite left.
The line of four pool tables, like a knife blade,
Slices the floor in half, ceiling beams parallel
To crouching tables, as if in collusion,
Gathering in close proximity at the back wall
Above the still door, with the explosive energy
Of discordant creatures unnaturally confined.
Above each table, a lantern dangles by a wire,
Like a spider lowering itself upon its prey,
Filament upon filament, inches at a time.
The left wall is bare, save for a rack of cues,
And an indecipherable sign, its block letters
Unaccountably blurred, poised as if containing
A last word on why the hall is so oddly empty,
Its atmosphere seemingly drawn up so tight
Even an echo couldn't travel but a few feet.
Why the tables crouch like wounded animals,
The room itself twisted with expectation,
Back door under pressure of an enormous wind.

The four men occupying the hall in the second
Look as if simultaneously aware of the sting
Of decay rising from discolored carpet,
Mildew rippling out toward the hall's corners,
Just reaching the feet of the closest player,
Who tenses as he discerns its clammy grip.
The two pairs seem oblivious to each other,
Separated by gulfs of age and knowledge,
Though all project a laborer's weariness,
All now looking toward the front of the hall,
As if someone they've dreaded has arrived,
Perhaps the foreman who daily terrorizes
With shouted curse word or slap of a fist,
Hobbled footsteps across concrete

Unmistakable in the dim echoes of the shop,
His bitter breath putrefying in the heat.
The players seem shocked at his showing,
The casual arrogance such a move betrays,
Determining his presence like mildew
In the air, with burning of nostrils.

The youth pretending manhood in the third
Pose on opposite ends of the second table,
Their anonymity shielded by the dim lantern
As if their presence is a security breach
(deftly slipping by the sleeping proprietor,)
As if any moment the working men would return
To sweep them like dust back in the street.
As if expecting it, they wear caps and coats,
Nervously absorbed in the game, or pretending,
One with his back turned away from the door,
The other bent but only to gauge his shot,
Yet with his bony back tensed like a spring,
Set to fly him in fear through the back door
Into the void of the alley, and his youth.
The sign on the wall, now clearly legible,
Looms up in stark detail, "Pay As You Go,"
Though they've not yet begun to understand
The distance they'll be required to travel,
Fighting twin urges to run and stay
Even as loud voices sound in the street
And the fat proprietor awakens from sleep.

Trophy

Few in the crowd
At the soccer game
On the edge of town
Near Bull Creek
Notice the dark figure
Rise above the far embankment,
Then descend into dense,
Uncut weeds.

Head down,
Hands in pockets,
He mechanically
Plows into brush
North of the field,
Heading toward town,
Footwork plodding,
Stiff as a stopwatch.

His head is bent as if
He sees a breakaway
And only he can take it in,
Invisible ball
Dribbling between
With each footfall.

Then he ducks
Into trees,
As if the starling
On the fencepost
Has whistled
Timeout.

When he returns
In the growing dark,
The crowd of parents
And exhausted players
Have since filed out
In trucks on the gravel path.

None to see his triumphant
Return, his pace more
Focused and relentless,
The trophy of a large bottle
In a paper sack tucked
Beneath his slack arm,

His other arm waving
To wind and birds,
As he strides atop
The embankment,
Too modest to take a bow,
Then disappears.

Cage Fighter

While her opponent dances
To burn off nervous energy,
She glares flat-footed

At the meager, wiry woman
With missing tooth and cobra
Tattoo on her left shoulder.

The gal looks haunted, hungry,
Frazzled. The kind of fighter
No one wants to face.

She bites her mouth guard
Until she feels it buckle.
The taste of plastic fills

Her mouth. She swallows
Five times to wash it down,
Then pounds her fists once,

After which the bell rings,
When both lunge
Like dogs pent up and whipped

Till they can't be contained.
The one who wins will sport
Fewer bruises, less blood.

The one who loses will call in
At the convenience store
Or factory for four days

Until her face resumes its
Approximate shape and size.
Until bruises turn yellow.

Until she can once again
Smile with the old swagger,
Bend down to tie her shoes,

Share images of the brawl,
Not think that this is all
There is, to be broken down

Like scrap metal and bent,
Burned, and blasted into
Something other, better.

Upper Deck

We feel sorry for those behind home plate,
So close their world is all details,
With nowhere to climb.

South wind sweeps across rows of seats up here
To connect us with worlds we cannot see,
To let us breathe.

The distance from the field, from the action,
Makes us scan about for meaning,
To hold back just so.

Open seating surrounding us dotted with folk
Assures us we will not be lost,
That few will infringe.

Blue sky unfurling above us like a giant flag
Reminds us not to swear allegiance
To that which is unchangeable.

Step after step like those of cathedral towers
Lead us after a win to the exit gate,
Breathless, alive, devout.

Ump

You change quickly after the game,
Become invisible.
On the way to your car,
No one accosts you.

Outside of the uniform your shoulders slump.
You have no gravitas.
No one would take your word on anything,
Even weather.

On Millfire Road, your car has a flat.
None of the five trucks that passes stops to help you.
You seem competent, kneeling in gravel.
Their churning tires acknowledge this.
They hurry home in the moonlight,
Screaming line drives.
Road is a cord that slowly tightens around your life.

Then you are alone, philosophical in the dark.
All the universe is a baseball game.
The moon is home plate.
That shooting star could be a home run.
Wheat lightly claps. An owl hoots.
Nothing to do but make your way home.
Where wind waits to slap your back,
The empty house to embrace you,
The bed to carry you all night
On its shoulders.

Rock Climbing in Horse Thief Canyon

We pull the boat ashore
Along a rock bank
Made up of fallen boulders
Scattered with frail beginnings of cottonwoods.
Our boots clatter along the stones,
Our hands caress brittle layers
Of shale deposits,
Engraved with fossils,
Which crumble at the softest touch,
Turn to dust.

The steep cliff,
Layers of millions of years,
Carefully preserved,
Slowly flakes away
Or falls in great blocks,
Shattering below.
Each stratum leads to another,
All the way to the tall weeds,
The overhanging elm,
At the bluff's summit.

We couldn't climb it,
Even with the proper gear,
We tell ourselves,
Stuck here at the bottom,
The lowest rung,
Primitive men,
Backs to water,
Eyeing those precarious crags.

Rebuilding Coach

You know you will lose.
Yet every motion,
Even the way you lift your cap
Then yank it down tighter,
Radiates authority, grit.

You pace like expected,
A caged tiger conjuring a bloodied gazelle.
You grip the clipboard like it was rope,
At the end of which you dangle
Above a fire pit.

You lower your head
And bark at your offensive coach
As if the team has done nothing right.
We should be four touchdowns ahead!

After the quarterback's fifth sack,
You freeze while you star-gaze,
Praying for clarity.
You hold position long as you dare,
Waiting for your quarterback to slink
To the sideline and become invisible.

When the final score is announced,
It echoes from the burning pyre
Of your disappointment, your rage.

No one speaks to you on the dark bus.
Your body barely acknowledges potholes.
Your shoulders square with contained fury.
Old artificer, you feign impatience
The way prairie pretends to be inviting,
Or trees pretend to be asleep,
Or darkness deep.

Bus Driver

Marge again,
Her window open,
Hair swirling
In late autumn breeze
Like a headful
Of angry snakes.

Marge, who doesn't joke much,
Whom the team first tried
To rib, then mostly let be.

Marge with bow legs
And a daughter somewhere
In Indiana with a pock-marked
Husband who cheats on her.

Road unrolls before her
Like gray, cracked linoleum.
Beyond the barbed fence
Are square miles of indoor,
Outdoor carpet.

When they arrive and the team,
Hustles inside steel doors,
She naps against the window,
Reads a romance novel chapter,
Watches that black cloud nearing,
And thinks about her father.

By the third quarter she sits
On the front row munching
Popcorn, sipping diet Coke.
Seven minutes to go she's
Warming up the bus.

"Ah, youth," she thinks,
"They can have it."
Her life now a succession
Of days like this—placid,

Small, attentive to the sky,
To the taste of rain.

After time,
Losses don't hurt so much,
She would tell them,
Even husbands who leave you,
Or children who die young.

Except sometimes on a dark road
When you're humming some old hymn
And staring at your reflection
In a bug-stained windshield,
The past leaps out
Into the light like a deer
And you swerve
Yet again.

Shadow Cyclist

He is not graceful
Like I imagined. Nor
Speedy. He lumbers,

Weighed down
And weary. He keeps
Pace though, headwind

Never veering him
Off course. Not bad
For riding astride

The ditch, for hitting
What by my count
Are eighty-seven

Light poles, nine
Stop signs, three
Mailboxes. As I crest

One hill he leaps
Inside his back tire
Like a hamster

Within a treadmill
Still running to keep
Spinning alongside

Me, then while I
Glance way, vaulting
Back onto the seat.

What an adventure
Seeker! What an athlete!
Of all people

To ride with on such
A sunny afternoon,
He chose me.

Fishing on the Kaw River Rule

One thing you must remember
If you're gonna stand on the banks
Of the Kansas River:

Fish, fish, if you will.
Let everyone see you smile
As you try to reel
In the big one. Just don't
Be too quiet about it
Though nobody wants you to yell.

Running Across Chase County, Kansas

Starting Line

Stretching beneath
The sign with two bullet holes,

I gauge gray sky,
Pulsing veins of darkness.

Swimmer

Wind rushes in
To fill space

Where sea water once
Raced for shore.

Specimen

All afternoon, incredulous
Farmers in trucks

Slow to ask if I
Need a ride, son.

Flint Hills

At the ridge top
Semis swoop past

Honking great blasts
Of pterodactyl breath.

Race Official

Wind whistles
A break through

Windows of
An abandoned house.

Diner Lunch

When I tell the waitress
I'm running across the county,

She says she's running too,
Out the door at five o'clock.

Rain Shower

I'm now walking
With my head down,

Rivulets
Pacing like blood.

Freedom

The old bull escaped
From the broken pen

Jogs a bit as I pass,
Vanishing into the ravine.

Gas Station Window

Plastic bottle under
The outdoor tap,

I watch a waterbug dash
Across the mirrored plains.

Exhaustion

My breath becomes
Some panting beast

Running beside me
Barking into wind.

Town

Suddenly land falls away
To reveal miles ahead

A sparse silent line of homes
With a sun shaft sprinting past.

County Line

I lean against the sign
For fifteen minutes while

Storm clouds inside me
Veer away into the hills.

IV. The Season Ends

Chicago Marathon—1999

For A.M., who died at age 36.

I imagine him nearing
The twenty mile mark,
Among a group of ten runners,

Heavy mist dulling sounds
Of their footsteps on Chicago streets,
Miles past the last conversation.

The body steadily resists his commands,
As it would again only two years later,
But for now he is winning the battle,

Lungs continue to pull in enough air,
Legs churning away in the damp cold,
Ankles absorbing shock after shock.

A camaraderie exists between these ten,
A brotherhood of exaltation and pain,
If only for a few moments before several

Begin to pull away around a sharp turn,
As he studies the backs of their heads
To memorize them for the years ahead.

Maybe that was his vision at the end,
Surrounded by such steadfast companions,
With only a few more miles left to run.

What Losing Sounds Like

Coach sits up till 2:30
With a percolating coffee pot for company.

Cottonwoods laugh merrily on the hill.
Nothing can keep those diehards down for long.

Even the slightest surge is cause for joy.
They're probably doing the wave even now.

Cattle, which have wandered to the meadow
North of the barn, mutter some local gossip,

Then, for the span of fifteen minutes,
Grow silent as the inside of a well.

That's the way with home crowds.
The herd mentality strikes again.

The football-shaped clock keeps on chugging
Like a locomotive on a steep upgrade.

He's the player every coach loves.
Maximum effort, even at the butt of his career.

Everyone knows he's winding down.
But those muscular arms just keep churning away.

Coffee pot keeps up a running commentary,
Rambling on about next week, next year,

An assistant coach till the end,
Trying to keep your spirits up, up.

I've got a surefire plan, coach,
He says. Listen to this.

Final Season of the Six-Man Red Dogs

Or the Vanishing Hometown

After tonight's blowout,
Trucks begin their awkward dance,
Ducking and faking
In search of a hole,
Then sprinting for open road,
Left arms out into the wind
As if to stiff-arm the night.

Even the surest, fleetest of mind
Might glance over shoulders
To see what might be lurking
On the edges of fields,
Having read our signs
In the huddle and countered
Every move, every reverse
In our thin, yellowing playbook.

Outside town,
Trees already losing leaves
Loom like linebackers
From the edge of headlights,
Lean, ripped,
Long arms reaching
To block us out,
To make us swerve,
To lose resolve.

We've been running this play
For so many years now—
Others carry the ball
While our hands grip
Nothing but air.

Above us stars flicker
As if there's a faulty connection
In the rafters,
Wiring gnawed by mice

Or frayed by time,
As we turn onto gravel roads,
Edging deeper into
Now whipping trees
And bent grass.

Stars have much to teach us
About fading away
With grace,
With strength,
Still shining.

Rodeo Clown

Crouched in the dirt,
The clown awaits the bull's
Release, his rage.

Red shirt
And blue overalls
Are his armor.

A rubber chicken
His lance.
A padded barrel

His castle.
After the gate explodes
And rider spins off

Into the dirt,
Bull stabbing air
With its horns,

He throws his pink bonnet
And deflects,
Distracts.

Nothing can blunt
Rage but
Misdirection.

Sleight of hand.
The snorting,
Spinning venom

Circumvented
By jumping jacks,
By running toward

It waving
A purple flag,
By the lewd,

Lascivious grin
Of a stretchable
Pullet hen.

1600 Meter Final: IA

Kansas State Track and Field Championships

Her small town is etched upon her face:
The look of her father when life disappointed him.
The echo of silence in an empty house.
The blank stare of window blinds hiding joy and pain.
The inscrutability of a rusted shed beside a burned out home.
The ache of an abandoned truck without wheels or doors.
The stoicism of Main Street with boarded-up stores.
The longing of wind through an un-mowed yard.
The furrowed brow of a cow pond when a storm wind breaks.
The tension of sparrows after a shotgun blast.
The ferocity of a stray dog to scraps of meat.
Scraps of meat and tendons and bone.

Radio Play by Play

From your table at the top of the stands,
You keep up a running patter.
For those listening out there
At kitchen tables,
In machine sheds,
From wobbly chairs at the town pool hall.

Sometimes your voice breaks through
The crash of chatter and pool balls,
Above footfalls across cracked linoleum,
Wind whistling through broken glass,
Above the whine of sanders,
Above the roar of silence.

Mostly not. Still reaching out
Through hedgerows and cattle pens,
Across tangled weeds in parking lots,
Sweeping dust from abandoned stores,
Sailing through dead grass,
Across frozen pastures,
Piercing the darkness
With knife-like waves.

Strip Pit Fishing II

I remember the leave-taking most of all,
Sitting in silence, mildewed vests
Snug against our chests, boots sloshing

In a half-inch of water, as the boat backtracked
Through dynamite- blasted canyon walls
Then in shadows. All was abandoned.

Several pieces of rusted-out machinery
Jutted out of thick brush and stone
Like petrified praying mantises,

Frozen in the act of reaching out
As if to examine something, to pull it
Close and turn it over and over to determine

If it was edible, and if so, then to eat it
Slowly, precisely. A twisted cottonwood
Sapling stood at the top of the north wall

After our last turn, a hunched, ragged
Local with rifle over shoulder,
Making sure we cleared out,

Right arm stunted, swinging
Uselessly in wind. Below not a breeze
Stirred. Nothing to dry cold sweat

On our foreheads that formed despite
The chill in the air, thick as wool.
Sloshing water was pungent as ether

In the bottom of the boat, with a tadpole
Rolling back and forth beneath my feet. Bass
And carp dangling on two stringers

Thumped against the side of the boat.
Ahead, we saw the truck impatient in grass,
Wheels dug into damp earth.

My dad powered down the outboard.
I lifted the stringers out of water,
As the fish came to life again, thrashing

Against chain links, gills heaving.
What compelled anything to fight to stay
In such a place, only the dark can say.

State Football Championship Fans

Road stretched before us like gray ribbon,
Taut, frayed and cracked.

The van, after a few missteps, settled into a rhythm.
Hills and pasture checkered with cattle unrolled

Thin, uneven carpet. Two cottonwoods on ridgetops
Launched what was left of their confetti. The detritus

Was gathered up by wind, old janitor
Sweeping willy-nilly while whistling a tuneless rag.

Hours from home, we would spot another hometown truck
Or car and marvel how large the world had become.

Our waves were like cottonwood leaves. Our hearts
Opened like canyons. Never mind the final score.

The pummeling at the hands of a superior force.
We prefer to remember that five-hour tunneling

Through chilly winds, sunlight on hilltops,
How prairie held us up and sustained us.

Playoff Momentum After a Lopsided Loss

It might have receded all afternoon,
Leaking from tailpipes of rusted pickups,
Dripping from leaves and guttering,
Evaporating like steam from cracked radiators,
Seeping into ground like tobacco spit,
Bouncing like droplets on hot stoves,
Shaken like dust from moldy carpets.

Now only absence,
Nagging like songs that can't be recalled,
Floating like affirmation never uttered,
Haunting like friends that won't reach out,
Like a spirit that reaches for your hand
That you can almost feel
But passes right through.

The Bus Ride Home

No one whispers
On the way home
After such a loss.

Gray frozen road
Cuts like a serpent
Through barren hills.

Headlights struggle
Ahead of the rattling bus
Like runners gasping for air.

No one wins in these Flint Hills
On a cold January night
Except darkness.

Besides numbness,
Players feel only rising
And falling of glacial drifts,

Ebbing and flowing
Of an ancient sea
Inside their chests.

Wind rattling windows
Once blew across waves
Writhing with creatures.

Battling for dominance,
They leaped out of darkness
And caromed back into spray,

Death cries
Echoing like thunder
Across the moonless night.

One player stirs from sleep
With such a bellowing cry
Rising from his diaphragm

But squelches it just in time,
Then turns to the window
And the undulating plains

With an uncomprehending gaze,
Unaware of the lesson about loss
Among ravines,

That after the struggle ends,
And all memory of victor
And vanquished disappear,

Swallowed by darkness,
Only wind will be left
To remember the sounds.

Chiefs Games

Sunday afternoons dad's cancer fight
Crescendoed with coin flips, referee whistles.
Weak from chemo, dad roared back
During games, knifing through depression
To talk how proud he was of my children,
To launch compliments like extra points,
Groan loudly at incompetence,
Roll eyes at the late score.

Maybe a plan still percolated beneath
The quarterback's ridged brow:
Helmet adjusted, jaw clenched,
Fist slammed into the opposite palm.
Perhaps I observed dad and sensed
Beyond fear, beyond exhaustion,
Plays improvised from a lack of options,
Offense backed up to the opposite end zone.

How could I not dream like a diehard fan,
Holding my breath and cursing the clock?

October

Wind through burnt grass,
Through scorched barbed wire posts,
Across stone-flecked ravines,
Against a black hawk's outstretched wings,
Above eyes of a fox peeking from a collapsed shed,
Through dried leaves gathered beneath a stone wall,
Brushing past the flagless pole beside a farmhouse,
Ripping away last leaves of a bent cottonwood,

Then blew across the trampled football field,
Across mud-flecked trucks in the parking lot,
Whipping banners twist-tied to the chain link fence,
Tearing away shouts of the quarterback,
Wrenching loose ends of the aging coach,
Shredding his nerve, his confidence,
Rending his defensive line frazzled,
Splitting everything he knows in two,

Before whistling past the water tower,
Through tangled brush beside the highway,
Knifing through cracks in pavement,
Testing rusted locks on pasture gates,
Spitting dust through broken windows,
Hissing through empty bottles,
Through rock bluffs along the creek,
Rattling cans and paper scraps.

The End

The turkeys' ease strikes us as they exit trees
Strutting with heads bobbing
Fanning out and pecking cornstalks
Bulldozed by recent combines.

Miniature dinosaurs striding deep ruts
Just before orange sky rains down
A screaming comet trail.

Like them, we might not be looking up.
We could be walking back from the creek
Barely speaking and comfortably so
In the bubble of our timeworn intimacy.

V. Post-Season

Post-Season

Football

Down forty to zero in the first quarter
Is like dealing with the lengthy illness

Of someone he loves—
Time to talk, laugh, and grieve.

Swimming

Still in the water waiting for the last
Competitor to touch the pad, she tastes

Unlike the champion that familiar trace of iron
And smoke on the back of the tongue.

Baseball

Worried that he's taking the playoff loss
Too hard, his father tracks him down

In the weeds behind the barn to find him
Constructing a fortress from plywood scraps.

Basketball

By late July and with still no word even from
Junior colleges, he attempts to piece together

Every second of what was now his last game—
High-fives, substitutions, cheers.

Golf

From her car window on the edge of the course,
She spots him alone on the fourteenth green

Bundled in a heavy coat putting with gloves on,
Then walking with head down against the wind.

Volleyball

What she learned was standing her ground.
One's territory is to be protected at all costs,

She reflects as she drives beyond fields
Into vast open country burned by sun.

Track and Field

He thinks as he rolls out of bed just before noon
One should have a tape at the conclusion

Of every challenge, with a timer to jot down
How well you did, and a coach to chew your butt.

Tennis

Each day after her final match she passes the court
And takes a quick glance to gauge the right time

To begin hitting balls, maybe testing her serve.
Today? No, definitely not today. Not quite yet.

Rodeo

Steak tastes better when it costs a broken arm
Or bruised hip. Even air is clearer as he now

Walks among horses against which he fought,
Tumbled, and cursed for seven long months.

Home Field

Cows graze on tender shoots
Near where the outfield fence stood.
A killdeer screams in the depression
Across which runners tried to reach home.
Hidden in the grass above what was the batter's box,
Her chicks tremble as air hums.
Robins tread this ground and bit by bit
Carry souvenirs back to nests.

The old farmer stands on that small rise where
Blurred by summer heat, phantoms sat side by side
In the dugout, or faces pressed to the fence,
Chanted, "Home run!" as he circled the bases.
Or marveled as he leaped to spear
Another line drive and snuff a rally.

He remembers neighbors, long since dead,
Used to drive by and shake their heads
While hunched in knee-deep grass,
He batted hedge apples
With a broken hoe handle.

"Home run! Home run!" he shouted
Over and over as startled birds rose
From hedge lines like cannon blasts
Of black confetti.

Black Ball Cap

Only days after his death,
All evidence of his illness—
Mattress pads, tissue box,
Tongue swabs, prescriptions—
Are removed in a garbage bag,
Black for mourning.

Hospice folds the adjustable bed.
The open morphine bottle
Is drained into a wastebasket.
Unopened bottles are chauffeured
To the sheriff's office.

His bureau is straightened.
Everything tucked away
Except sorrow
Scattered about the floor,
Leaking in through closed windows.
Like marbles, it presses
Through dress shoes.
Its torn envelopes
Lie scattered in my chest.

We do what we can to tidy up.
Now if only the black ball cap
On the nightstand
Could forget the shape
Of his head.

Bike Race

Thirteen ghost bikers jockey for position
Inside my late father's bike shop.

So far Black Phantom is winning,
Sleek, built for intimidation.

Whatever race is being ridden
Has lasted now over thirteen months.

Distance may not be the measure,
For it snakes through a landscape

Of spinning dust motes and fusty air.
A droning yellow jacket is the cop keeping

Everything under control, hovering near
Red Schwinn as if to tell him to straighten up,

We run a tight race in these parts. These parts
Being a shed which was once a chicken house.

Black Phantom leads but can't break away,
Can't sustain a charge. The others are drafting in

His wake, as if the finish line were just beyond that
Locked door, just one sustained downhill run away,

The race wrapping up rather than picking up speed,
Turning the last corner rather than endless. Eternal.

Tossing Stones

Once a coach,
Always a coach,
You tell all the fellows
At the Country Café.

You drill waitresses how to do their job,
Charge up the wife when she's down,
Note moves of sun and stars,
Chew out death at funerals.
Not afraid to get in his face
For crossing the line.

For years you were the assistant coach
To your replacement. Now you note
With some satisfaction that he stoops
And shuffles like you on the sidelines,
Stares at stars after a botched play,
Just like you,
Fumes internally until the clock expires,
After a loss until he drives the pickup
Past cornfields to pond's edge
And skips rocks until one o'clock.

But what good does it serve?
You mutter as you take another sip
Of lukewarm coffee. Boys, the wins
Are never quite as good as you think.
The losses, well,
One can get a lot of thinking done
Tossing stones. Barking at the moon.
Falling asleep in the truck cab
Listening to coyotes howl.

Russell Field

The uniform was bleached white, stiff—
Garment of fear, of belonging.

The world was letting me try it on briefly—
Too long in the arms, too short in the legs.

Outliers sat at the end of the bench,
Played right field, were sent to bat

Only when politic. Guaranteed outs.
The ball was small yet fierce, relentless,

Unlike me. After games, cold pop
Was handed out like celebratory champagne.

Faces have been rubbed out,
But the sky was cornflower blue.

I remember the concrete dugout,
The rusty faucet dribbling on the floor,

Cracked wood benches layered with dust,
Sparrow droppings, the chain link fence

Through which I looked out onto the field
Like an animal caged by its own inadequacy.

I'm grateful all these years, the field now
An empty lot, for learning how to look out

Onto the world—cracked sky, parched grass,
Sagging left field fence, faded water tower—

Lean forward against links,
Then spit.

Walking the Field after Last Night's Win

Tramped-down grass has yet to uncoil.
Wind has cleared its breath of all crowd noise
Except sighs caught in the fence.
Speakers above the press box can only
Whisper and hiss when a crumpled program
Stutters into the end zone.

The game is distilled to a stirring in air,
Salt of evaporated sweat on a grass blade.
A beetle scaling a mound of bare earth,
Cleat marks steadily unmarking themselves,
Tension in the seats still unclenching.

I walk one more revolution,
Steps measured and appreciative,
To mourn the echo,
And by the time I enter the car,
The echo of an echo of an echo.

Legacy

". . .a collection of more than 200 baseballs signed by Negro Leagues players . . .. [is] the largest . . . of its kind in the world and one of the most popular exhibits at the [Negro Leagues Baseball] *museum"* -- Kansas City Star

Perhaps he took it out of the box,
A pristine baseball—cork, yarn, leather—
And just sat with it, gripping it again and again
After so many years, feeling how it fit his hand,
Rubbing his gnarled thumb across stiches
As if nursing an old wound, scar tissue thick
And raised, finally digging in several fingernails
To hold it steady in front of his weathered face so that
Eyes could adjust, grasping this as it were
All he had left of his playing days, his legacy,
Pausing for the blast of a train through the window,
His unsteady pen then gliding across leather,
Fierce strokes of anger and resentment leavened
By graceful whorls of acceptance, of pride,
Before returning it to the box,
In silence, sensing it still in his grip,
Staring at his knuckles.

Driving Range: Web.com Tour

The aging pro fires blast
After blast into the void
With ferocity, with control,

Face maintaining calm,
Behind which his eyes appear
Unsettled, even haunted.

Will he find his game again,
From out of humid air,
Trees, blue sky, his gut?

Will windows of expensive
Homes adjacent to the course,
Rather than offer reflection,

A sense of rightness and peace,
Serve only a vision of the present
Burnished with what used to be?

Perhaps his actions are too hurried,
Reaching for tees or additional balls,
To suit our small, attentive crowd

Who remember his name if not
His face, who sense in the moment
As we pause on our way to hole 15

Some level of human drama playing
Out as he sheaths driver abruptly
And scowls as he takes up an iron.

Perhaps grass offers him solace,
The world to which he has pledged
Everything shallow and deep.

He reaches for a dropped towel
And momentarily lingers,
Caressing a tuft of spindly grass.

Does wind only taunt him,
Questions swirling around his face
Like dried leaves inside a storm?

Does earth shift with every step,
So that he leans to left or right,
Hoping that hills remain solid?

Perhaps everything lost shall be
Restored, for him, for us all,
If we just keep taking our cuts.

Or maybe he offers real wisdom
When he slices another iron into
The bag, and mutters, "Screw it."

Globe

It lay behind the outfield fence
Like an apple
On the orchard floor.

Careful of the soft spot
On the underside near the seam,
Discolored, mushy.

This fruit will keep the doctor away.
This apple will sit on your desk
And ape the roundness of your world.

Sent spinning by your son's bat,
By the fullness of his fledgling heart,
Soul following it into right field.

In a square glass case,
It will stare at you on winter days
Like an eye with cataracts.

It will look on you with sympathy,
But as a shadowy figure
Bending down from fog.

All that it has absorbed
It conceals beneath layers
Of cork, rubber, thread.

No world is seamless
With eighty-eight inches of thread
And one hundred eight stitches.

You will take it out
And breathe it deep
Like an exotic cigarette.

Dirt, sweat,
Leather burned by years,
And summer heat.

A coworker will enter
To find you spinning
A stitched globe.

Rodeo

The cheers of the crowd
Their easy banter
Echo in silent waves

Across the rodeo arena
Gray and frozen
Under a winter sky.

Last July's extravaganza
Was well-attended
But this crowd is infinite!

Bullish and expectant,
Wind tears
At chute gates.

Riding the air,
Bucking and rocking,
A snowflake hits the dirt.

In the corral,
Leaves skitter
Like nervous colts.

An empty bag
Bloated and brash
Staggers for the exit.

A loose cord
On the ticket booth
Waves more in.

Weeds tick them off,
One at a time,
On a chain-link fence.

No need for tickets
Or hand stamps
Or life.

Fleet of Foot

The trophy you never got
Doesn't sit on the mantel
Or shelf above your desk.

Sunlight reflecting off it
Will never star your eyes
Nor halo your face.

Your children won't
Ask to touch it, hold it,
Nor hear the story—again.

You won't favor one leg
From the muscle tear
Suffered to acquire it.

The old nightmare of tripping
In front of the finish line
Won't ever wake you.

When failure bites,
You won't visualize it
To maintain perspective.

When success shouts,
You won't compare it
And find today lacking.

Your spouse will never
Have to live up to it,
Life's greatest moment.

Some days will never
Seem lonely or bitter
Or sad as a result of it.

Cheers won't echo
Nor trees applaud it
When you jog at dawn.

No one will look at you
With envy or resentment
At what they never won.

You will not feel the need
To put it away so that
Visitors won't scorn it.

Holding it over your head
Like a wreath of laurels,
Filling it with champagne

And raising a quick toast,
Will never occur to you
When in the house alone.

Souvenir Baseball

You were fouled into general admission seats,
A low screamer from the first baseman's bat.

Striking an empty seat, then bouncing straight up,
You found the fingers of an old man, plucking you

From the air like a low hanging peach,
One scuffed by the bat above the seams, damp

From pitcher's spit, ridged by his fingernail,
Now splashed with beer as two men nearby

Toast you by clinking plastic cups and shouting.
You are not pristine but were only thrown once.

Your place in the game is minimal, the batter
Striking out next pitch, then slinking into the dugout.

You were his fifth straight foul but the hardest hit.
Your energy cannot be denied. Even now the fan

Turns you over and over in his hand, eyes
Dancing, raising you over his head as if you were

Too bright and too hot to be so near his face.
Even in his jacket pocket your power sears.

Demolition Derby Car

It sits in tall weeds
Like a crushed, jagged brain.

No beat or synapse pulses
Where it sits behind the shed.

All is unnaturally calm the way
Operating rooms are after everything

Has been tried, the surgeon has backed
Away and removed her mask, nurses

Disconnect all life-sustaining devices,
All silent except for clanking of tools

Being placed on trays and wheeled away.
Soon the patient is lifted onto a gurney

To be awaited by mourners, those for whom
The body is all they have and so they can't let

It go. Not yet. So now he has wheeled this corpse
Into waving September grass to await eternity.

Only a few birds care to mourn. Tree limbs
Lean down to caress hollowed-out eyes

Which look unseeing into darkening prairie,
Where wind and sky collide time after time.

Before a raucous crowd of jays.

Thomas Reynolds is an English professor at Johnson County Community College in Overland Park, Kansas, and has published poems in various print and online journals, including *New Delta Review, Alabama Literary Review, Aethlon-The Journal of Sport Literature, The MacGuffin, Flint Hills Review, Sport Literate, Spitball: The Literary Baseball Magazine,* and *Prairie Poetry*. Woodley Press of Washburn University published his poetry collection *Ghost Town Almanac* in 2008. His chapbook *The Kansas Hermit Poems* was published in 2013, and his sports-themed chapbook *Small Town Rodeos* was published by Spartan Press in 2016. He enjoys cycling, running, and golfing.

www.ingramcontent.com/pod-product-compliance
Lightning Source LLC
Chambersburg PA
CBHW032128090426
42743CB00007B/508